# GET ACTIVE!

# BAT AND BALL SPORTS

Barbara C. Bourassa

First published in the United States by
QEB Publishing, Inc.
23062 La Cadena Drive
Laguna Hills, CA 92653

www.qeb-publishing.com

Library of Congress Control Number: 2007000933

ISBN 978-1-59566-350-4

Written by Barbara C. Bourassa
Edited, designed, and picture researched by
    Starry Dog Books Ltd
Consultant Steven Downes, of the Sports Journalists'
    Association www.sportsjournalists.co.uk

Publisher Steve Evans
Creative Director Zeta Davies
Senior Editor Hannah Ray

Printed and bound in China

Web site information is correct at time of going to press.
However, the publishers cannot accept liability for any
information or links found on third-party Web sites.

All the sports in this book involve differing degrees of
difficulty and the publisher would strongly advise that
none of the activities mentioned are undertaken without
adult supervision or the guidance of a professional coach.

Words in **bold** can be found
in the Glossary on pages 30–31.

Picture credits
Key:
T = top, B = bottom, C = center, L = left, R
= right, FC = front cover, BC = back cover

S = Shutterstock.com, C = Corbis,
D = Dreamstime.com, G = Getty Images,
BSP = Big Stock Photo.com, ISP =
iStockphoto.com

Credits:
FC (main image) G/ © Jim Cummins,
(top to bottom) S/ © SI, S/ © Alexander
Kalina, S/ © Glenda M. Powers, S/ ©
Alan C. Heison, S/ © Larry St. Pierre, S/
© MAT, S/ © Steve Cukrov.

1 S/ © Sonya Etchison; 4 S/ © Alan C.
Heison; 5 (top to bottom) S/ © MAT, S/
© SI, S/ © Alexander Kalina, S/ © John
Barry de Nicola; 6t C/ © Michael St.
Maur Sheil, 6b C/ © Nik Wheeler; 7 C/
© Royalty-Free; 8t S/ © Graca Victoria,
8b S/ © Phil Anthony; 9 D/ © Freefly;
10t S/ © Lance Bellers, 10bl S/ © Jason
Merideth; 11 G/ © Jim Cummins; 12b
C/ © Liu Liqun; 13c C/ © Mark Gamba,
13bl ©2007 ITTF Museum, all rights
reserved, www.ittf.com/museum; 14bl
S/ © Lori Carpenter; 15 C/ © Brownie
Harris; 16c C/ © Bettmann, 16bl S/
© Andrea Catenaro Doherty; 17 S/ ©
Larry St. Pierre; 18t Skijornow.com/ R.
Briggle, 18bl S/ © James M Phelps,
Jr; 19 D/ © Christophriddle; 20t D/ ©
Webking, 20b S/ © Steve Cukrov; 21cl
D/ © Christophriddle, 21cr S/ Riddle
Photography; 22t C/ © Reuters, 22b S/
© Alexander Kalina; 23tl D/ © Dshawley,
23c C/ © Eliana Aponte/Reuters; 24
C/ © Ariel Skelley; 25bl S/ © Norliza
binti Azman, 25c D/ © Slinscot; 26t S/
© Kamarulzaman Russali, 26b ISP/ ©
Lance Bellers Photography; 27 C/ © Roy
McMahon; 28t ISP/ © Uzinusa, 28b C/
© Royalty-Free; 29 G/ Stockbyte.
BC S/ © Peter Weber.

# CONTENTS

IN THE world of sports, there are many different activities that use some type of bat (or stick) and ball. You might choose to hit tennis balls over a net with a racquet, or you may enjoy learning how to sink balls with a pool cue. There's a bat and ball sport to suit every personality!

## Plenty of choice

If you like playing on a team, consider lacrosse or field hockey. If you prefer an individual sport, tennis may be the game for you. If you like fast action, try table tennis. If a slower pace with sudden spurts of activity is more your style, you could try baseball. Whatever sport you choose, they are all fun, easy to learn, and a great way to make new friends!

*Some female lacrosse players wear cage-like face guards to protect their eyes during a game.*

## TIME AND PATIENCE

Before you head for the field, court, or course, there are a number of things to keep in mind. Remember that many of the players you see on TV or at live events are professionals with years of experience (and practice). So don't expect to be as good as they are right away! Learning any new sport takes time and patience, and it's best to focus on having fun, rather than trying to master every little detail of your chosen sport.

## Protect yourself

Many bat and ball sports require protective gear, such as helmets and pads, for the body or face. Lacrosse players, for instance, usually wear heavy padded gloves to protect their hands, and most cricket players wear helmets and pads. Such protective equipment for your head and body can prevent injuries if you bump into another player, are hit by a ball, or slip and fall down.

## Practice makes perfect

As any good **coach** will tell you, learning a new sport means understanding and mastering the basics. You'll need to take good care of your equipment and practice a lot. All sports, from golf to table tennis, keep you healthy and active. Remember to drink plenty of water, eat well, and take breaks whenever you need to. Most sports also involve a certain amount of danger. But when they are played correctly, they're all fun, so turn the page for the lowdown on some bat and ball sports!

# LACROSSE

LACROSSE is an exciting game that was invented by First Nations/Native Americans. The modern game is played by two teams of 10 (men) or 12 (women). The players use lacrosse sticks, called crosses, to move a hard rubber ball around a field. They use the mesh pockets at the ends of their sticks to scoop the ball off the ground and pass it to other players, who catch it and pass it using their sticks.

## Aim of the game

Lacrosse is similar to soccer in that the players run back and forth trying to get the ball into the other team's goal. The attackers line up close to the opponent's goal and try to score. The defenders stay near their own goal to defend it from the other team's attackers. As in soccer, each team's goalkeeper stays close to his or her goal to guard it from the other team's players.

### WHAT IS HURLING?

Hurling is thought to be the oldest field game in Europe. It is an Irish game similar to lacrosse. The stick (or hurley) and ball (or sliothar) resemble those used in field hockey. Two teams of 15 players hit the ball on the ground or in the air, and a player can pick up the ball with his or her stick and carry it for four steps.

### Lacrosse on horseback

Polocrosse is a sport that combines lacrosse and **polo**. Players carry sticks that resemble lacrosse sticks, but they ride horses like in a game of polo.

◄ In polocrosse, two teams of six players play the game on horseback.

## Protective gear

Lacrosse players wear helmets to protect their heads, and on their hands they wear large, padded gloves. There's a lot of running involved, so if you want to try lacrosse, get ready to work your leg muscles!

*The French named the early lacrosse sticks "crosses," because they looked like a bishop's staff, called a "crosse."*

### DID YOU KNOW?

Lacrosse is played at the international level by 26 countries and the Iroquois Nationals. The Iroquois is a group of First Nations/ Native Americans mainly from eastern Canada and the northeastern USA. They are the only First Nations/ Native American team allowed to compete in international sport.

### LEARN MORE

Visit these lacrosse-related Web sites:
- www.lacrosse.org
- www.laxlinks.com

# TENNIS

TENNIS is fun and easy to learn. All you need to play is a racquet, a ball, a net to hit the ball over, and someone to play against. A large, rectangular court is generally used, either indoors or outdoors.

## What to wear

It used to be that tennis clothing had to be white, white, and whiter. Today, however, tennis outfits have changed. It's not unusual to find tennis players wearing red, blue, pink, or even black outfits.

### TENNIS TALK

You will need to buy, rent, or borrow a tennis racquet if you want to play tennis. The "grip" is the area of the tennis racquet that you hold onto, or grip. The "head" is the part of the racquet that hits the ball. Strings across the head form a grid of netting off which the ball bounces.

## Who's who in tennis

Because tennis is so popular, its best players are often well known to many people. In the United States, Andy Roddick is widely recognized. Roger Federer of Switzerland is a multiple winner at major competitions, such as Wimbledon and the US **Open**. Among female tennis players, Maria Sharapova of Russia, Amélie Mauresmo of France, Serena Williams of the United States, and Kim Clijsters of Belgium have many loyal fans.

◀ Maria Sharapova was born on April 19, 1987 in Siberia, Russia. She is 6' (1.82m) tall, and is one of the world's best tennis players.

## Where to play

If you want to learn tennis, there are many ways to do so, from group or individual lessons to tennis camp or tennis clubs. Tennis can be played outdoors on **asphalt**, clay, or grass courts, or indoors at a sports center. In some parts of the world, outdoor tennis courts are roofed over in the winter with stiff domes of plastic called bubbles so players can play all year round.

➥ *Tennis is often played in the summer on outdoor courts. Players wear shorts or short skirts and lightweight shirts to keep cool.*

## FAMOUS COMPETITIONS

Tennis is popular all over the world, and many people like to follow the game (and the players) by attending competitions such as the US Open, the French Open, or the Australian Open. If you can't get to a live event, you can follow the action on television. During the two weeks of the summer when Wimbledon is shown on TV, the streets often seem much emptier!

## Singles and doubles

There are two main ways of playing tennis. In a singles game there are just two players, one on each side of the net. In a doubles game there are four players on the tennis court, a team of two (called a pair) on each side of the net. In both types of games, only one ball is hit back and forth. The court is marked with outer sidelines and inner sidelines. Doubles players can hit the ball to the outer lines and singles players use the inner ones.

## Racquetball and squash

The games of squash and racquetball are related to tennis. Both involve hitting a rubber ball around an indoor court. In tennis, if the ball is hit outside the court it is considered out of bounds, but in racquetball and squash you can hit the ball off the walls as well as the floor. Both squash and racquetball can be played as a singles game or a doubles game.

| GAMES | POINTS |
|-------|--------|
| 3 | 30 |
| 2 | 40 |

### GAME, SET, MATCH

The scoring system in tennis is quite complicated. Tennis is played in a sequence of **games** that are scored using points. At least six games make up a **set**, and generally two or three sets (but it can be as many as five) make up a **match**.

◀ *A racquetball is slightly larger than a squash ball, and the racquet has a shorter handle.*

### BADMINTON BASICS

Badminton is similar to tennis, except everything is a different shape! The racquets are lighter, the court is smaller, the net is taller, and instead of hitting a ball back and forth, players hit a small cone called a "shuttlecock" or "bird." Badminton became an Olympic sport in 1992, when Indonesia, South Korea, and China won most of the medals.

## Try, try, and try again...

If you are learning tennis, you will probably do lots of practice exercises designed to help improve your skills. Your coach may stand close to the net, for instance, and send over practice balls for you to return. Another easy way to practice tennis is to hit the ball against a wall.

### OLYMPIC TENNIS

At the 2004 Olympic Games in Athens, China won its first gold medal in tennis. Li Ting and Sun Tiantian beat a pair (team) from Spain for the top honors in the women's doubles.

## Stop and start

Tennis is a game of movement. Because the ball can be hit anywhere on the court, you'll need to run after it. Learning to run after the ball and then slow down enough to hit it back over the net can take some practice.

▶ *When serving, the player stands behind the baseline, throws the ball up into the air, and hits it over the net into the service box diagonally opposite (marked by white lines on the ground).*

# TABLE TENNIS

**T**ABLE TENNIS is a fast and exciting game in which two players use small paddles to hit a hard plastic ball over a low net strung across a table. The players take turns serving for two points in a row. The first player to get 11 points (with a two-point lead) wins the game. When the server hits the ball, it must bounce on the server's side of the net first and then on the opponent's side before it is returned. The game requires great speed, and is fun both to watch and to play!

**DID YOU KNOW?**
Table tennis has precise rules. The International Table Tennis Federation (ITTF) states an official table tennis ball must be white or orange and weigh 0.1 ounces (2.7g).

◆ Ping-pong is popular with children all over China. These schoolchildren from the Guangxi Zhuangzu region are playing on a table made from a piece of concrete, with a line of bricks for a net.

▶ World champion table tennis players come from all over. Many of the world's best players are from China and South Korea.

## What is ping-pong?

Ping-pong is another name for table tennis. It is the term generally used when the game is played just for fun by children. Most people agree that the name came from the "ping" and "pong" noises made by the ball in the days before paddles had foam cushions.

## Getting started

To play table tennis you need a few basic pieces of equipment: a paddle (or racquet), a ball, a net, and a table. In international competitions the net must rise exactly 6 inches (15.25cm) above the table. At home you don't need to be so precise. Instead of a net you could use a piece of fabric, or even a row of tin cans!

### DID YOU KNOW?

In Switzerland, there is a museum of table tennis (see www.ittf.com/museum/). Why not try out its simulated game on your computer? Check it out at: http://www.ittf.com/games/game.htm

# BASEBALL

**B**ASEBALL is an American pastime. To get a game going, you need only a ball, a bat, and a few friends to play with. You might also want a glove for catching the ball and a hat to keep the sun out of your eyes.

## Pitcher and catcher

In an organized game of baseball, two teams of nine players take turns at bat. The game starts when the **pitcher** throws the ball to the **catcher**. The catcher crouches behind **home plate**, one of four **bases** on the field. The other team's batter, standing in a marked area on one side of home plate, attempts to hit the ball so that he or she can run around the four bases and score **runs**.

### GET YOUR GLOVE

There are many different types of baseball gloves. It's important to buy the right kind of glove for the position you are playing. If you are just getting started, you'll need a basic fielder's glove for catching.

## Scoring runs

If the batter hits the ball, he or she must run to first base. (The batter becomes a **runner**.) The batter can either stop there or run to the next base. If the batter runs continuously around all four bases without being thrown or tagged **out**, he or she scores an inside-the-park **home run**. The team with the most runs wins.

◆ *Before taking a swing at the ball, the batter holds the bat at a 45 degree angle over his or her back shoulder. He or she must keep the eye on the ball in order to hit it.*

## The four bases

The main area of the field in which a game takes place is called the diamond. In the center is the pitcher's mound, where the pitcher stands to throw the ball to the catcher at home plate. The corners of the diamond are marked by the four bases. First, second, and third base are each guarded by a **fielder** called a **baseman**, who is ready to catch the ball.

### DID YOU KNOW?

Baseball is thought to have developed in the mid-1700s from the English game of **rounders**. In rounders, two teams of nine players take turns batting and fielding the ball. The batter scores a "rounder" by running past each post before the other team's fielders can "tag" or touch the posts with the ball.

➡ *This baseball game is being held at the Rogers Center in Toronto, Canada. The stadium is unusual because it has a huge roof that can open and close over the whole field. It seats 51,517 fans at baseball games.*

## Fielding positions

In an organized game, there are nine players on the field at any one time. The infielders include the pitcher, catcher, first baseman, second baseman, third baseman, and short stop (who plays between second and third base). Outside the diamond, at the greatest distance from the batter, are the outfielders, which include the left fielder, center fielder, and right fielder. All fielders must be good at catching and throwing.

## Girls and baseball

Although many people think baseball is a male sport, plenty of girls like to play, too. In many parts of the USA, 10- to 12-year-old girls play alongside boys on their baseball teams. Some girls also like **softball**, a game similar to baseball but which uses a larger ball.

➥ *You can take a tour or even have a birthday party at Yankee Stadium, home of the New York Yankees.*

## Starting young

In the USA, kids as young as four or five might play T-ball, a game in which the ball is hit off a T-shaped stand. Older children can play baseball and softball games organized by **Little League**.

## World-famous Yankees

The New York Yankees are probably the best-known baseball team in the world. The reason? They have won the **World Series** 26 times! The World Series is a competition between the winners of the two leagues that make up **Major League Baseball** in the USA and Canada.

## Worldwide appeal

Many baseball players from all over the world go to the USA to play. The Dominican Republic, Cuba, Japan, and Puerto Rico are all well known for their baseball stars. On the streets of the Dominican Republic, children play baseball almost all year round. One of the most famous players in Major League Baseball is Sammy Sosa, from the Dominican Republic.

### COOPERSTOWN

The Baseball Hall of Fame is in Cooperstown, New York. Taking a trip there to learn about famous baseball players such as Babe Ruth, Ted Williams, and Joe DiMaggio (left) is a fun adventure for many children (and their parents). You can visit the hall of fame online at www.baseballhalloffame.org

When batting, baseball players wear helmets to protect their heads. They also wear cleats, which give good grip when running.

**T**HE GAME of golf involves using various clubs to hit a small ball into a set of 18 holes scattered around a course. Along the way are obstacles such as lakes, sand traps (bunkers), trees, and rough grass. The player who hits his or her ball into the 18 holes using the smallest number of strokes wins.

**Talented Tiger**

Tiger Woods is one of the world's best players. He has won many major golf tournaments, including the **Masters** four times, the British Open Championship three times, and the US Open twice.

➡ *This man is using a **putter** to hit his golf ball into the hole, which is marked with a flag.*

➡ *Tiger Woods started playing golf at the age of two. He hit his first **hole in one** at the age of six.*

**GOLF CLUBS**

Golf players carry a variety of clubs, each designed for a different purpose. Most clubs can be grouped into one of three categories: **woods**, **irons,** or putters.

## Which club to use?

A player starts a game by hitting the ball for a long distance from a special area of the course called the **tee**. To hit the ball long distances, most people use a club called a "wood" or "driver." The driver has a large, rounded head designed to hit the ball as far as possible. As the player gets closer to the hole, he or she will probably use clubs called "irons." These tend not to hit the ball as far as woods and are used for more accurate shots. Once the ball is on the green—an area of very short grass where the hole is located—the player uses a "putter" to hit the ball into the hole.

### WELL-KNOWN WOMEN GOLFERS

Golf is a great game for girls, some of whom go on to become top-earning professional women golfers. Michelle Wie did so when she was just 15 years old. Two other world-famous women golfers are Annika Sorenstam of Sweden and Lorena Ochoa of Mexico.

◀ *Many golfers wear a glove on one hand to help them grip their clubs.*

## Worldwide appeal

Golf has been played for at least 500 years in the UK, though its origins are uncertain. Today it is played all over the world on courses that use the natural environment—streams, lakes, hills, and trees—to add difficulty to the golfer's game. But it can be played anywhere. It was even played on the Moon, where astronaut Alan Shepard, on lunar mission Apollo 14, played a shot that he said went for "miles and miles" because of the low gravity!

Miniature golf, also called putt-putt, is a popular pastime with tourists at beach resorts.

## Miniature golf

Young children may enjoy miniature golf. The player uses a putter to move the ball through and around various obstacles—such as model windmills —in as few strokes as possible.

## Where to learn golf

There are many places to learn golf. Many large golf courses offer junior lessons. There are also golf clubs, golf camps, and golf outings to choose from. Most golf courses have a resident pro, or golf expert, who will give advice to new players.

On a **driving range**, golfers spend many hours practicing how to stand and how to hold and swing the club to hit the ball.

## Extra equipment

Golfers wear special gloves to provide grip and shoes with spikes to stop them from slipping as they take shots. In their bag they also need golf balls and "tees." A tee is a small, Y-shaped piece of wood or plastic on which the ball sits when the player **tees off** at the start of each hole.

◀ *Having hit the ball, the player "follows through" with a swing.*

### DID YOU KNOW?

Some golf courses that are next to the ocean are called "links." One of the most famous is Pebble Beach (left) in California. It overlooks the Pacific Ocean. In Ireland, Ballybunion is beside the Atlantic.

# FIELD HOCKEY

FIELD HOCKEY in its modern form was first played in the mid-1700s by schoolchildren in England, and it is still popular with children. Play usually takes place on a rectangular field, where the players are arranged in similar positions to those on a soccer field—there are attackers, defenders, and a goalkeeper. Using wooden sticks, the players pass the ball up and down the field and try to hit it into the other team's goal.

## A team game

There are 11 players on a field hockey team. As in soccer, **passing**, **marking**, and **tackling** are important aspects of the game. The field hockey stick itself is just under 3.3 feet (1m) long. It is similar to an ice hockey stick, but the head—the area used to hit the ball—is smaller.

**OLYMPIC ALL-STAR**
Field hockey has been part of the summer Olympic Games since 1908. One of the most successful players of all time is Rechelle Hawkes (above) of Australia. She has won three Olympic gold medals.

◀ A penalty corner is a type of play that allows one team to try and score from near the goal. They get this chance because the other team has fouled. Five players from the defending team must stand behind the back line until the ball has been hit.

## STICK FACTS

The head of a field hockey stick has a rounded side and a flat side. The flat side is used to hit the ball.

## FIELD FACTS

Most outdoor field hockey is played on artificial turf fields that measure 100 yards (91.4m) long by 60 yards (55m) wide. The goal at each end is 7 feet (2.14m) high and 12 feet (3.6m) wide. Around the goal there is a D-shaped area known as the **shooting circle**.

Field hockey involves a lot of tackling by opponents. Players are only allowed to hit the ball with the flat face of the stick.

## Basic equipment

If you want to play field hockey, you'll need shin guards, a stick, and a ball. The shin guards are to protect your lower legs from the impact of the ball or another player's stick. In schools, field hockey is often played on grass, so cleats provide grip. At recreation centers and elsewhere, however, synthetic surfaces are more popular and sneakers should be worn. Some field hockey players also wear mouth guards to protect their teeth and goggles to protect their eyes.

## Street hockey

Street hockey is closely related to field hockey and ice hockey. It is basically the same game, but is played on paved surfaces such as a street or rollerblading rink. The players wear sneakers or rollerblades, and use ice hockey sticks instead of rounded sticks.

### ICE HOCKEY

Ice hockey is a fast-paced, exciting game similar to field hockey, but played on ice with ice hockey sticks and a puck (a smooth-sided, solid, thick disc). The players wear heavy pads and helmets to protect themselves from sticks, flying pucks, stray ice skate blades, and checks.

➤ *There can be as many as 16 players in a street hockey team, but 10 of them will be reserves. Only six members of the team take part in the action at any one time.*

**FIELD HOCKEY** CONTINUED 2

A flying field hockey ball travels fast and is very hard, so the goalkeeper protects his or her body and face with extra padding and a helmet.

## INDOOR HOCKEY

In indoor field hockey, the number of players, the rules of the game, and the size of the field are all different from outdoor field hockey. Instead of 11 players on a team, there are 6. The players cannot hit the ball, as in outdoor field hockey. Instead, they push, scoop, or flick the ball into the goal.

# CRICKET

CRICKET is popular in many countries, especially the UK, India, Sri Lanka, South Africa, Pakistan, Australia, and the West Indies. Once you've mastered the basics, it's a great game to play.

## Playing the game

In cricket, two teams of 11 players take turns batting and fielding. The game is played on a field that includes a long, narrow section called the pitch. At each end of the pitch is a set of stumps and bails (an arrangement of three upright sticks topped by two smaller sticks) called a **wicket**. The batsman stands in front of the wicket and tries to hit the ball to prevent the bowler (on the other team) from hitting the wicket with the ball. A second batsman (on the same team as the first) stands by the bowler's wicket. To score a "run," the batsman hitting the ball must run and change places with the other batsman.

### PROTECTIVE GEAR AND EQUIPMENT

A cricket ball is very hard, so most cricket players wear equipment to protect their hands, face, and legs. The wicketkeeper, for instance, wears leg pads to protect his shins and heavy gloves to protect his hands. The batsmen wear helmets with face grills, arm guards, leg pads, and gloves.

## Team effort
Other people on the field include fielders, two umpires (who enforce the rules), and the **wicketkeeper**. Each team's turn at the wicket is called an **innings**. The team that scores the most runs wins.

◄ *Bowlers try to make the ball hard to hit. Some balls are bowled very fast. Others bounce and curve in an unexpected direction.*

## TWENTY20 CRICKET

Twenty20 is a shortened form of cricket that takes about three hours to play. By comparison, a Test match—a game between two national teams—may take up to five days to complete. In Twenty20 cricket, the players often wear brightly colored clothes (instead of white).

▸ *A batsman uses a wooden (traditionally willow) paddle-like bat to defend the wicket.*

### DID YOU KNOW?

A professional cricket ball weighs between 5.5 ounces (155.9g) and 5.7 ounces (163g), about the same as a baseball. Balls for children and women are smaller.

POOL is played on a rectangular table with pockets at the four corners and in the middle of each long side. Sixteen balls are used: seven red ones, seven yellow ones, one black one, and a white **cue ball**. Sometimes, players use seven solid-colored balls (numbered 1 to 7), the black 8-ball, and seven striped balls (numbered 9 to 15). Using a stick called a cue, the player hits the white cue ball, which in turn knocks one of the other balls into a pocket.

## WHAT IS SNOOKER?

Snooker is similar to pool, but is played with 22 balls: 15 red ones (worth 1 point each when sunk) and six other-colored ones. They are yellow (worth 2 points), green (3 points), brown (4 points), blue (5 points), pink (6 points), and black (7 points), and a white cue ball. To score, players must "pocket" all the red balls first, then the colored balls. The black ball is sunk last.

## Cue clues

A cue is usually made of wood and is slightly thicker at one end. The narrow end has a leather tip and is used to hit the white cue ball. Most pool players use chalk on the tip to improve contact between the stick and the ball.

*Chalking the leather tip of a pool cue helps the player hit the ball with greater accuracy toward the hole because it stops the cue from skidding off the ball.*

## Whose turn?

The players have one set of balls each—either a color (the reds or yellows), or the spots or stripes. They each try to sink all their balls into the pockets before the other player. If a player sinks the correct ball, he or she has another turn. If he or she fails to sink a ball, the opponent has a turn. In most games, the black ball must be sunk last.

▶ *To judge what angle and strength to hit the cue ball, it helps to look down the length of the cue so you can line up your shot.*

### THE SPORT OF KINGS?

Many famous rulers, including Mary, Queen of Scots and Napoleon Bonaparte, loved playing billiards (from which snooker and pool were developed).

**asphalt** A smooth, paved surface.

**base** Square marker used in baseball to mark three of the four points of the baseball diamond. (Home plate is the fourth.)

**baseman (baseball)** A fielding position; the first baseman plays on first base, the second baseman on second base, etc.

**catcher (baseball)** The player who catches the ball thrown by the pitcher.

**coach** An instructor who works with players to improve their game.

**cue ball** The white ball used to hit other balls in snooker and pool.

**driving range** A place for golfers to practice hitting and driving.

**fielder** A player whose job is to catch or stop the ball and return it.

**game (tennis)** A match is made up of a series of games. A game is won when one player, or pair, scores at least four points and is more than one point ahead of the opponent(s). (The first point is called 15, the second is 30, the third is 40, and 40-all is called deuce. The next person to score has the "advantage." If the player with the advantage wins the next point, he or she wins the game. If he or she loses it, the score goes back to deuce.)

**hole in one (golf)** A shot that enters the hole from the tee.

**home plate (baseball)** The base that runners must reach to score a run.

**innings (cricket)** Each team's turn to bat at the wicket.

**inside-the-park home run (baseball)** A run scored when a batter runs continuously around all four bases without being thrown or tagged out.

**iron** A type of golf club generally used for accurate shots taken between the tee and the green.

**Little League** A US organization that manages baseball and softball leagues for children all around the world.

**Major League Baseball** The organization that oversees professional-level baseball in the USA and Canada.

**marking** When a player on one team stays close to a specific player on the other team in order to make it difficult for him or her to pass or receive the ball.

**Masters** A major golf tournament played each year in the USA.

**match (tennis)** A tennis match consists of between two and five sets. A set includes at least six games.

**Open** A competition (as in the US Open in golf and tennis) which nationally top-rated athletes, either amateur or professional, may enter.

**out (baseball)** The batter is out if he hits the ball and a fielder catches it before it hits the ground; if a baseman catches the ball before the runner reaches his base; or if the batter swings three times and fails to hit the ball.

**passing** When a player hits or kicks the ball to another player.

**pitcher** The baseball player who throws, or pitches, the ball over home plate towards the batter and the catcher. The batter tries to hit the ball before it reaches the catcher.

**polo** A game in which players riding horses use mallets to hit a ball into goal.

**putter** A flat-sided golf club used on the green to hit the ball into the hole.

**rounders** A game in which two teams of nine players take turns batting and fielding the ball, and running around four posts to score rounders.

**run** In baseball, when a player runs around all three bases and crosses home plate. In cricket, when a batsman hits the ball and runs to the other wicket.

**runner (baseball)** Once the batter is on base, he or she becomes a runner.

**set (tennis)** A tennis match consists of between two and five sets. To win a set, a player or team has to win at least six games, and at least two games more than their opponent(s)—for example, six games to four or seven games to five.

**shooting circle** The semicircular area in front of a field hockey goal. Shots on goal must be made from within the circle.

**softball** A game similar to baseball that uses a larger ball and is played on a smaller diamond.

**tackling (field hockey)** When a player runs up to another player and places his or her hockey stick in the path of the ball to gain possession of it.

**tee, tee off** The tee is the place on a golf course from which the ball is struck (teed off) at the beginning of play for each hole.

**wicket (cricket)** Three upright poles (stumps) with two smaller sticks (bails) on top. There is a wicket at each end of the cricket pitch—the central strip where the batsmen run.

**wicketkeeper (cricket)** The player who stands behind the wicket and catches the ball bowled by the bowler (if the batsman does not hit it).

**wood** A type of golf club used to hit the ball off the tee or for long distances.

**World Series** The annual competition between the top two Major League Baseball teams.

## WEB SITES
**Lacrosse:** www.lacrosse.org
www.laxlinks.com
**Table tennis**: http://www.ittf.com/ games/game.htm
**Baseball:** www.baseballhalloffame.org